MASTER YOUR GADGETS

ULTIMATE GADGET PERSONALIZATION: 120 EXPERT TIPS FOR A UNIQUE TECH LIFE

ANAND M
AMEENA PUBLICATIONS

MASTER YOUR GADGETS

DEDICATION

To the Visionaries in My Professional Odyssey

This book is dedicated to the mentors and leaders who guided me through triumph and adversity in my professional universe. Your guidance has illuminated the path to success and taught me to seize opportunities and surmount obstacles. Thank you for imparting the advice to those who taught me the value of strategic thinking and the significance of innovation to transform obstacles into stepping stones. Your visionary leadership has inspired my creativity and motivated me to forge new paths.

Thank you for sharing the best and worst of your experiences with me, kind and severe employers. As I present this book to the world, I am aware that you have been my inspiration. All of your roles as mentors, advisors, and even occasional adversaries have helped me become a better professional and storyteller.

This dedication is a tribute to your impact on my journey, a narrative woven with threads of gratitude, introspection, and profound gratitude for the lessons you've inscribed into my story.

With deep gratitude and enduring respect,
Anand M

FROM TECH TO LIFE SKILLS – MY EBOOKS COLLECTION

Dive into Anand M's rich collection of eBooks, curated meticulously across diverse and essential domains.

Pro Tips and Tricks Series: *Empower yourself with life-enhancing skills and professional essentials with our well-crafted guides.*

Hot IT Certifications and Tech Series: *Stay ahead in the tech game. Whether you're eyeing certifications in AWS, PMP, or prompt engineering, harnessing the power of ChatGPT with tools like Excel, PowerPoint, Word, and more!, we've got you covered!*

Essential Life Skills: *Embark on a journey within. From yoga to holistic well-being, Master the art of culinary, baking, and more delve deep and rediscover yourself.*

Stay Updated & Engaged: *For an entire world of my knowledge, tips, and treasures, follow me on Amazon*
https://www.amazon.com/author/anandm

Your Feedback Matters!

Your support, feedback, and ratings are the wind beneath my wings. It drives me to curate content that brings immense value to every aspect of life. Please take a moment to share your thoughts and rate the books.

https://www.amazon.com/author/anandm

Together, let's keep the flame of knowledge burning bright!

Best Regards,
ANAND M

HOW TO USE THIS BOOK

Welcome to "Master Your Gadgets: 120 Advanced Customizations & Hacks." By selecting this guide, you've already taken the first step towards mastering your electronic devices in ways you never thought possible. Congratulations on embarking on this exciting journey! Get ready to dive deep into a world of technological marvels that will not only enhance the functionality of your gadgets but also give them a personal touch that speaks volumes about who you are.

Why This Book is a Must-Have
In today's digital age, we are surrounded by an ever-increasing array of gadgets. They assist us, entertain us, and sometimes even define us. These devices have become an extension of our personality. So, why settle for generic settings and designs? Your devices should reflect your uniqueness and style, and this book is your gateway to making that happen. Think of this guide as your personalized roadmap to standing out in the tech-driven world.

Stand Out and Lead
Each
CHAPTER in this book presents curated tips and tricks that will set you apart. The strategies herein aren't just about aesthetics— they're about creating a user experience that's uniquely you. Whether you want your phone to have that perfect boot-up animation or your camera gear to reflect your style, there's something here for everyone. By applying these hacks, you won't just be another face in the crowd. You'll be the trendsetter, the go-to person for all things tech-customization. Others will wonder, "How did they do that?" And you'll have this book to thank for that edge.

Practice Makes Perfect
While the hacks and customizations in this guide are designed to be user-friendly and accessible, remember that practice is key.

Some might require a few tries to perfect, but don't get discouraged. The more you engage with each tip and trick, the more adept you'll become, and soon, customizing gadgets will feel like second nature.

Your Quick Reference Guide
For those moments when you need a quick refresher or are looking for a specific hack, don't forget to refer to the table of contents. It's your shortcut to diving straight into the wealth of knowledge contained within these pages, ensuring that you're always ready to impress.

Personalize and Innovate
While this book offers a comprehensive compilation of expert tips, it's also an invitation for you to innovate. As you familiarize yourself with these customizations, think about how you can tweak or expand on them. Your personal touch, combined with the foundational knowledge from this book, can lead to creations that are truly groundbreaking.

Embark on a Transformative Journey
We believe that this book, with its expert insights and curated advice, will be an invaluable resource for you. But remember, it's not just about following instructions—it's about embracing a mindset of innovation, personalization, and excellence. With "Master Your Gadgets" in hand, you're not just a user; you're a creator, a trendsetter, a tech maestro.

So, gear up for a transformative experience. Dive in, explore, experiment, and most importantly, enjoy the journey of mastering your gadgets. Here's to making every device truly yours!

CONTENTS

CHAPTER 1 - LAPTOP AND COMPUTER ENHANCEMENTS

TIP 1: PERSONALIZED KEYCAP REPLACEMENTS

Category
Laptop and Computer Enhancements

Brief
Replace your standard keyboard keycaps with custom-designed keycaps to give your laptop a unique and personal touch. Not only will it make your keyboard stand out, but it can also enhance your typing experience by choosing keycap materials and designs that suit your preferences.

Steps
1. Identify the keycaps you want to replace.
2. Purchase custom keycaps or design your own.
3. Use a keycap puller to remove the old keycaps.
4. Carefully place the new keycaps on the switches. 5. Press firmly to secure them in place.

Practical Challenges
- Finding compatible keycaps for your laptop model can be a challenge.
- Some keycap sets may not align perfectly with all keyboard layouts.

Tactics to Overcome
- Measure your laptop keyboard layout accurately.
- Check for keycap compatibility with your laptop model.
- Consider a universal keycap set and adjust as needed.

TIP 2: CUSTOMIZING THE BIOS BOOT LOGO

Category
Laptop and Computer Enhancements

Brief
Change the default BIOS boot logo to something more personal or customized. This modification adds a unique touch to your computer's startup process. You can use your favorite image or design something specific for this purpose.

Steps
1. Access the BIOS settings during boot (usually by pressing a key like F2 or Del).
2. Navigate to the boot options.
3. Locate the setting for changing the BIOS boot logo.
4. Upload or select your custom image/logo. 5. Save and exit the BIOS settings.

Practical Challenges
- *Changing the BIOS settings can be risky if done incorrectly.*
- *Not all computers support this customization.*

Tactics to Overcome
- *Research your computer's BIOS capabilities.*
- *Follow manufacturer guidelines for BIOS customization.*
- *Be cautious and backup important data before making changes.*

TIP 3: CREATING YOUR OWN SCREENSAVER ANIMATIONS

Category
Laptop and Computer Enhancements

Brief
Design and create your own screensaver animations to display on your computer when it's idle. This adds a personal and creative touch to your workspace and can even serve as a source of inspiration during breaks.

Steps
1. Use animation software or tools to create your screensaver animation.
2. Export the animation in a compatible format (e.g., .gif or .scr).
3. Access your computer's screensaver settings.
4. Choose the custom animation as your screensaver. 5. Adjust settings like delay and duration.

Practical Challenges
- *Creating animations can be time-consuming, and compatibility issues may arise with certain file formats.*

Tactics to Overcome
- *Choose a simple animation style for easier creation.*
- *Use widely supported file formats like .gif.*
- *Test the screensaver on your computer to ensure compatibility.*

TIP 4: UNIQUE DIY LAPTOP SKINS

Category
Laptop and Computer Enhancements

 **Brief**
Personalize your laptop by designing and creating your own custom laptop skin. This not only protects your laptop from scratches but also showcases your unique style and creativity.

Steps
1. Measure your laptop's dimensions accurately.
2. Design your custom laptop skin using design software or templates.
3. Print the design on high-quality vinyl or skin material.
4. Cut the skin according to your laptop's shape. 5. Apply the skin carefully, starting from one edge and smoothing out any air bubbles.

Practical Challenges
- Getting the measurements and application right can be tricky, and removing air bubbles may require patience.

Tactics to Overcome
- Use a ruler or template to ensure precise measurements.
- Apply the skin slowly and carefully to avoid wrinkles and bubbles.
- Seek help from a professional if you're unsure about the process.

TIP 5: ORGANIZING CABLES WITH CUSTOM LABELS

Category
Laptop and Computer Enhancements

Brief
Tired of tangled and unidentifiable cables on your desk? Create custom labels for your cables to keep them organized and easy to identify. This not only reduces clutter but also saves time searching for the right cable.

Steps
1. Identify each cable and its purpose.
2. Create labels using label maker or printable labels.
3. Attach labels to both ends of the cables.
4. Use cable organizers or clips to keep cables tidy. 5. Ensure labels are visible and legible.

Practical Challenges
- Labels may wear out over time, and identifying very similar cables can still be a challenge.

Tactics to Overcome
- Use durable and high-contrast labels.
- Update labels if they become illegible.
- Color-code cables for easy identification.

TIP 6: TOUCHPAD GESTURE CUSTOMIZATION

Category
Laptop and Computer Enhancements

Brief
Customize touchpad gestures to suit your specific needs and workflow. This can greatly improve your navigation and productivity on your laptop.

Steps
1. Access your laptop's touchpad settings.
2. Explore the available gesture options.
3. Customize gestures by assigning specific functions or actions.
4. Test and adjust sensitivity settings if needed. 5. Save your custom touchpad settings.

Practical Challenges
- Configuring touchpad gestures may take some time, and not all laptops offer advanced customization options.

Tactics to Overcome
- Start with essential gestures like three-finger swipes.
- Experiment with different gestures to find what works best for you.
- Check for software updates that may offer more gesture options.

TIP 7: CUSTOM MOUSE CURSORS

Category
Laptop and Computer Enhancements

Brief
Elevate your cursor experience by creating or downloading custom mouse cursors. These unique designs can add personality and style to your computer usage.

Steps
1. Find or create custom cursor files (usually in .cur or .ani formats).
2. Access your computer's mouse settings.
3. Navigate to the cursor settings.
4. Browse for and select your custom cursor files for various cursor actions. 5. Apply and save your custom cursor settings.

Practical Challenges
- Not all cursor designs may be compatible with your operating system or cursor settings.

Tactics to Overcome
- Use cursor designs that are comfortable to use.
- Keep backup cursor files in case of issues.
- Ensure compatibility with your OS version.

TIP 8: TAILORED SYSTEM SOUNDS FROM PERSONAL RECORDINGS

Category
Laptop and Computer Enhancements

Brief
Replace default system sounds with custom ones created from your personal recordings. This adds a personal touch to your computer's audio feedback.

Steps
1. Record or collect audio clips you want to use as system sounds (e.g., your voice for notifications).
2. Access your computer's sound settings.
3. Browse for the specific sound events (e.g., new email notification).
4. Assign your custom audio clips to these events. 5. Adjust volume levels as needed.

Practical Challenges
- Finding suitable audio clips and ensuring they are in the right format can be challenging.

Tactics to Overcome
- Use clear and distinct audio clips.
- Convert audio files to compatible formats if needed.
- Test the sounds to ensure they're not too loud or too soft.

CHAPTER 2 -SMARTPHONE PERSONALIZATION

TIP 9: ANIMATED BOOT ANIMATIONS

Category
Smartphone Personalization

Brief
Boot animations greet you every time you switch on your smartphone. Customizing it can give your device a personal touch, setting the mood every time it's powered on. Imagine booting your device to see an animation of your favorite cartoon character dancing. It's especially fun if you love showcasing your phone's uniqueness to friends. This trick can make your daily device interaction delightful and personalized.

Steps
• Research device compatibility.
• Backup device data.
• Download a boot animation creator or suitable GIF.
• Apply using root access or dedicated apps.

Practical Challenges
Some phones might not support changing boot animations. Risk of device malfunctions if done incorrectly.

Tactics to Overcome
Always backup your device. Use verified apps and follow trusted tutorials. If unsure, consult tech-savvy friends or online communities.

TIP 10: DIY PHONE CASES

Category
Smartphone Personalization

Brief
With a DIY phone case, you can design a case that resonates with your personality or mood. Perhaps you want a case with beads, glitter, or even a photo collage of cherished memories. Creating one adds sentimental value and ensures your phone stands out. It's especially handy if you're tired of generic cases and desire a unique look. Plus, it's a conversation starter!

Steps
- Choose a clear phone case.
- Gather materials (e.g., photos, beads, paint).
- Design your layout.
- Secure items using glue/sealants.
- Allow time to dry.

Practical Challenges
Items might dislodge with wear and tear. The design might not be as polished as store-bought ones.

Tactics to Overcome
Use strong adhesive like Mod Podge. Consider using sealant for added protection. Practice designs on paper first.

TIP 11: PERSONALIZED APP ICONS

Category
Smartphone Personalization

Brief
App icons are the first thing you see on your phone's home screen. Personalizing them creates a harmonized aesthetic. Want a minimalist black and white theme? Or vibrant neon colors? Custom icons can revamp your phone's look, making daily navigation enjoyable. Plus, it harmonizes your phone's theme to your liking, enhancing the user experience.

Steps
• Download an icon pack or design your own.
• Use apps like Nova Launcher or Shortcuts (iOS) to apply.
• Adjust other UI elements to match.

Practical Challenges
Some apps may not have custom icons available. Might take time adjusting to new icons.

Tactics to Overcome
Use popular apps with vast icon libraries. Initially, label icons till you get accustomed. Over time, remove labels for a cleaner look.

TIP 12: NFC TAGS PROGRAMMING

Category
Smartphone Personalization

Brief
NFC tags are small stickers that store data. By programming them, you can automate tasks. Imagine tapping your phone on an NFC sticker next to your bed to activate 'night mode' - Wi-Fi off, alarm set, and phone muted. It streamlines routine tasks, saving time and ensuring consistency. It's highly beneficial if you have recurring device tasks throughout your day.

Steps
• Purchase NFC tags.
• Use NFC tools app to program desired actions.
• Place tags at strategic locations.
• Tap phone to activate.

Practical Challenges
NFC tags might not work if placed on metal surfaces. Tasks might not always activate correctly.

Tactics to Overcome
Test tags after programming. Place in easily accessible spots. Regularly update tasks as routines change.

TIP 13: CUSTOM VOICE NOTE RINGTONES

Category
Smartphone Personalization

Brief
Ringtones set the tone (pun intended!) for incoming calls or notifications. Using a voice note, like your child's laughter or a personal message, can be endearing. It's especially lovely hearing a familiar voice or sound that brings joy. Also, it ensures you don't mistake your phone's ringtone for someone else's in a crowd.

Steps
• Record or choose a voice note.
• Convert to ringtone format if needed.
• Set as ringtone via phone settings.

Practical Challenges
Voice notes might not be loud or clear enough. Accidentally using personal or sensitive voice notes.

Tactics to Overcome
Ensure recordings are clear. Use apps to enhance sound quality. Regularly change or rotate ringtones to keep them fresh.

TIP 14: AR BACKGROUNDS

Category
Smartphone Personalization

Brief

AR backgrounds offer an interactive smartphone experience. Imagine your wallpaper coming alive, like fish swimming on your screen or clouds floating. It brings vibrancy and interactivity, making each interaction novel. It's a must-try for those looking to elevate their phone's visual experience and impress friends.

Steps
• Download AR wallpaper apps.
• Choose or design an AR theme.
• Apply via the app or phone settings.

Practical Challenges
Some AR backgrounds can be battery-draining. Not all phones support AR functionalities.

Tactics to Overcome
Choose lightweight AR wallpapers. Use them on occasions rather than daily to save battery. Ensure your phone is AR-compatible.

TIP 15: CUSTOM WIDGET MANAGEMENT

Category
Smartphone Personalization

Brief
Widgets offer quick information or functions without opening apps. Customizing them ensures they align with your phone's theme and provides required info efficiently. For frequent phone users, tailored widgets streamline daily tasks and enhance the phone's visual appeal, creating a harmonized look.

Steps
• Decide needed widgets (weather, calendar, tasks).
• Use apps like KWGT to customize.
• Place on home screen and resize as needed.

Practical Challenges
Overloading screen with widgets might slow phone performance. Widgets might not update in real-time.

Tactics to Overcome
Limit the number of widgets on the home screen. Regularly refresh widgets to ensure they display updated info.

TIP 16: UNIQUE WALLPAPERS VIA PHOTO-EDITING

Category
Smartphone Personalization

Brief
A wallpaper can set your phone's mood. Using photo-editing apps, you can design unique wallpapers – perhaps a family photo with a vintage filter or a favorite quote on a scenic backdrop. This trick adds a personal touch, ensuring every time you unlock your device, it resonates with personal memories or aesthetics.

Steps
• Choose a base photo.
• Use apps like Snapseed or VSCO to edit.
• Apply effects, filters, or text.
• Set as wallpaper.

Practical Challenges
Over-editing might reduce image quality. Might not fit all screen sizes perfectly.

Tactics to Overcome
Always start with high-resolution photos. Ensure the main subject isn't hidden by app icons. Adjust as per phone's resolution.

CHAPTER 3 - WEARABLE TECH TWEAKS

TIP 17: SMARTWATCH FACE DESIGN CREATION

Category
Wearable Tech Tweaks

Brief
Design your own custom watch faces for your smartwatch to match your style and preferences. This allows you to have a unique and personalized look on your wrist.

Steps
1. Determine the specifications and requirements for your smartwatch's watch face design (e.g., dimensions, file format).
2. Use watch face design software or apps to create your custom watch face.
3. Customize elements such as background, watch hands, complications, and colors.
4. Test the watch face on your smartwatch and make adjustments as needed. 5. Save and set your custom watch face as the default.

Practical Challenges
- Limited compatibility with certain smartwatch models and operating systems.
- The learning curve for watch face design software.

Tactics to Overcome
- Check your smartwatch's compatibility with custom watch faces.
- Start with simple designs and gradually add complexity.
- Explore online communities for watch face design tips and templates.

TIP 18: CUSTOM ALERT VIBRATIONS ON FITNESS BANDS

Category
Wearable Tech Tweaks

Brief
Customize the vibration patterns and intensities for different notifications on your fitness band. This allows you to distinguish between various alerts without checking your device.

Steps
1. Access your fitness band's settings or companion app.
2. Locate the notification settings or vibration customization section.
3. Create or select custom vibration patterns for specific notifications (e.g., calls, messages, alarms).
4. Adjust the intensity and duration of each vibration. 5. Save your custom vibration settings.

Practical Challenges
- Not all fitness bands offer advanced vibration customization.
- Ensuring that custom vibrations are easily distinguishable can be challenging.

Tactics to Overcome
- Research fitness bands that support advanced vibration customization.
- Test and fine-tune custom vibration patterns to make them distinctive.
- Combine vibration patterns and LED colors (if available) for better notification differentiation.

TIP 19: PERSONALIZED WORKOUT ROUTINES ON WEARABLES

Category
Wearable Tech Tweaks

Brief
Create and customize your workout routines directly on your wearable device. This allows you to have tailored fitness programs that match your fitness goals and preferences.

Steps
1. Access the workout or fitness app on your wearable device.
2. Explore the option to create or customize workouts.
3. Define your workout parameters, including exercise types, duration, repetitions, and rest intervals.
4. Save your custom workout routine with a descriptive name. 5. Start your personalized workout directly from your wearable.

Practical Challenges
- Limited availability of workout customization on some wearables.
- Ensuring that custom workouts align with your fitness goals and needs.

Tactics to Overcome
- Research wearables that support workout customization.
- Consult with a fitness professional for guidance on designing effective workouts.
- Gradually increase the intensity of custom workouts as you progress.

TIP 20: HANDCRAFTED BANDS AND STRAPS

Category
Wearable Tech Tweaks

Brief
Design and create your own bands or straps for your wearable device. This not only adds a personal touch but also allows you to choose materials that suit your style and comfort.

Steps
1. Measure your wrist to determine the band size.
2. Select suitable materials for your band or strap (e.g., leather, fabric, silicone).
3. Cut and shape the material according to your wrist size and desired design.
4. Attach closures, clasps, or connectors to secure the band. 5. Install your custom band on your wearable device.

Practical Challenges
- Crafting custom bands may require some sewing or craftsmanship skills.
- Ensuring the band is securely attached to the wearable.

Tactics to Overcome
- Practice basic sewing or crafting skills before attempting intricate designs.
- Consider using tutorials or guides for creating custom bands.
- Double-check the attachment mechanism to prevent accidental detachment.

TIP 21: UNIQUE CHARGING DOCK DESIGNS

Category
Wearable Tech Tweaks

Brief
Create customized charging docks or stations for your wearable devices. These unique designs can enhance your charging experience and keep your devices organized.

Steps
1. Determine the specific requirements for your wearable's charging dock (e.g., charging port type, dimensions).
2. Choose materials and design elements for your dock (e.g., wood, acrylic, LED lighting).
3. Craft or assemble the charging dock according to your design.
4. Ensure that the charging connector aligns correctly with your wearable. 5. Test the charging dock with your wearable to confirm functionality.

Practical Challenges
- Crafting or assembling a charging dock may require tools and skills.
- Ensuring that the charging dock is compatible with your wearable's charging connector.

Tactics to Overcome
- Seek tutorials or guides for creating custom charging docks.
- Use readily available materials and components to simplify the process.
- Test the dock with your wearable before finalizing the design.

TIP 22: CUSTOM NOTIFICATION SOUNDS

Category
Wearable Tech Tweaks

Brief
Personalize the notification sounds on your wearable device. This allows you to associate specific sounds with different types of alerts, making it easier to identify them without looking at your device.

Steps
1. Access the notification settings on your wearable device or companion app.
2. Explore the option to customize notification sounds.
3. Select or upload audio files for different types of notifications (e.g., messages, emails, alarms).
4. Adjust the volume and vibration settings for each notification.
5. Save your custom notification sound settings.

Practical Challenges
- *Not all wearables offer advanced notification sound customization.*
- *Choosing and creating distinct notification sounds can be challenging.*

Tactics to Overcome
- *Research wearables that support notification sound customization.*
- *Use unique and easily distinguishable audio files for different notifications.*
- *Test the sounds to ensure they're not too loud or too soft.*

TIP 23: TAILORING ON-DEVICE STORAGE FOR TRAVEL

Category
Wearable Tech Tweaks

Brief
Optimize your wearable's storage for travel by selecting and syncing only the necessary apps, music, or data. This helps conserve space and ensures you have access to essential information while on the go.

Steps
1. Review the apps and data stored on your wearable device.
2. Identify the apps or content you'll need during your travels.
3. Delete or uninstall unnecessary apps and data to free up space.
4. Ensure that important travel-related apps and data are up to date and synced. 5. Test your wearable's functionality with the reduced content to confirm everything works as expected.

Practical Challenges
- Ensuring that you don't delete essential apps or data.
- Maintaining a balance between available storage and essential content.

Tactics to Overcome
- Create a checklist of essential apps and data before deleting anything.
- Prioritize syncing travel-related apps and content.
- Regularly back up your wearable's data before making significant changes.

TIP 24: DESIGNING PROTECTIVE CASING FOR RUGGED ENVIRONMENTS

Category
Wearable Tech Tweaks

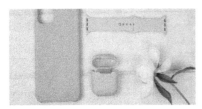

Brief
Create custom protective casings or enclosures for your wearable devices, especially if you plan to use them in rugged or challenging environments. These casings can shield your devices from damage.

Steps
1. Assess the environmental challenges your wearable will face (e.g., water, impact, dust).
2. Choose materials suitable for your protective casing (e.g., silicone, hard plastic, waterproof coatings).
3. Design or select a casing that fits your wearable snugly while allowing access to essential features.
4. Assemble or install the protective casing on your wearable device. 5. Test the casing to ensure it provides adequate protection without hindering functionality.

Practical Challenges
- *Designing and crafting a protective casing that balances protection with functionality.*
- *Ensuring that the casing doesn't interfere with sensors or features.*

Tactics to Overcome
- *Research existing protective casings and adapt them to your needs. Test the casing's fit and functionality thoroughly before relying on it in challenging environments.*
- *Prioritize protection but ensure it doesn't compromise usability.*

CHAPTER 4 - PERSONALIZING HOME ASSISTANTS

TIP 25: CUSTOM VOICE COMMANDS FOR EVERYDAY ROUTINES

Category
Home Assistants

Brief
Customize voice commands to automate daily tasks, like setting up a "Good Morning" command to adjust lights and provide updates. This adds convenience and personalization to your smart home.

Steps
1. Access your home assistant's settings for voice commands.
2. Create new voice commands, ensuring they're distinct from default ones.
3. Set up actions for each command.
4. Test and fine-tune your custom commands.

Practical Challenges
- Practical Challenges: One challenge may be ensuring that your custom commands don't conflict with default ones or are not too similar to avoid confusion. Another challenge could be adapting to using these new commands seamlessly in your daily routine.

Tactics to Overcome
- Tactics to Overcome: To avoid conflicts, choose unique phrases for your custom commands that are unlikely to be triggered accidentally. Practice using these commands regularly until they become a natural part of your interactions with your home assistant.

TIP 26: PERSONALIZED ANNOUNCEMENTS AND GREETINGS

Category
Home Assistants

Brief
Customize your home assistant's greetings and announcements for a warm and personalized touch. Make it greet you with a tailored message when you arrive home.

Steps
1. Access the settings for announcements and greetings on your home assistant.
2. Create personalized messages for different scenarios.
3. Set up triggers for these messages (e.g., arrival at home).
4. Test and refine your personalized announcements.

Practical Challenges
- Practical Challenges: One challenge is ensuring that the announcements match specific situations accurately and consistently. Another is maintaining a variety of personalized greetings to keep them fresh and engaging.

Tactics to Overcome
- Tactics to Overcome: To address the first challenge, test your announcements in various scenarios to fine-tune the triggers. Update messages as needed to keep them relevant. For the second challenge, periodically review and update your personalized greetings to avoid monotony.

TIP 27: CREATING AMBIENT SOUNDS FOR DIFFERENT MOODS

Category
Home Assistants

Brief
Generate ambient sounds through your home assistant to create the desired atmosphere for various occasions, such as calming rainforest sounds for relaxation.

Steps
1. Access the sound settings on your home assistant.
2. Explore the library of ambient sounds available.
3. Choose a sound that suits your mood or situation.
4. Adjust volume and duration settings as needed.

Practical Challenges
- Practical Challenges: Finding the right balance between sound volume and mood can be a challenge. Another challenge is ensuring that the sounds don't become repetitive over time.

Tactics to Overcome
- Tactics to Overcome: Experiment with different sound options to discover your favorites. Create playlists of ambient sounds to avoid repetition. Adjust the volume and duration of sounds based on the room's acoustics and your comfort level.

TIP 28: CUSTOM LED LIGHT SEQUENCES

Category
Home Assistants

Brief
Personalize your smart lighting by programming custom LED light sequences. Set up unique lighting effects for different events or moods, like colorful lights for parties.

Steps
1. Access your home assistant's lighting controls.
2. Create custom lighting sequences with specific colors and patterns.
3. Assign triggers or voice commands for these sequences.
4. Test and adjust the lighting effects.

Practical Challenges
- Practical Challenges: One challenge is syncing the lighting with various events or activities effectively. Another challenge is avoiding overwhelming or overly flashy lighting that may not suit every occasion.

Tactics to Overcome
- Tactics to Overcome: To address the first challenge, plan your lighting sequences for specific events in advance. Seek feedback from family members or guests to refine your lighting choices. For the second challenge, consider creating different lighting presets for different moods and activities, ensuring they are not excessively bright or distracting.

TIP 29: PROGRAMMING UNIQUE ALARMS AND REMINDERS

Category
Home Assistants

Brief
Customize alarms and reminders with your own voice or messages. Wake up to a personalized morning message or receive reminders in your own voice.

Steps
1. Access your home assistant's alarm and reminder settings.
2. Create new alarms or reminders.
3. Record your voice or add personalized messages.
4. Set the schedule for these custom alarms. 5. Test and adjust the alarms and reminders.

Practical Challenges
- *Practical Challenges: One challenge may be maintaining consistency in responding to personalized alarms, as they are different from standard alarms. Another challenge is ensuring that you don't oversleep due to personalized wake-up messages.*

Tactics to Overcome
- *Tactics to Overcome: To address the first challenge, gradually adapt to the new alarms to ensure they wake you up effectively. Combine personalized alarms with traditional ones as a backup until you are confident in the new alarms. For the second challenge, set backup alarms with standard tones to ensure you wake up on time, especially if you're still getting used to personalized wake-up messages.*

TIP 30: TAILORED FAMILY TRIVIA GAMES

Category
Home Assistants

Brief
Create customized trivia games for family entertainment. Personalize questions and themes to make game nights more engaging and enjoyable.

Steps
1. Access the trivia game settings on your home assistant.
2. Create custom questions and answers.
3. Choose themes or categories for your trivia game.
4. Set up game rules and scoring. 5. Invite family members to play.

Practical Challenges
- Practical Challenges: One challenge is ensuring that the questions are challenging but not too difficult, as the game should be enjoyable for all family members. Another challenge is maintaining family interest in the game over time.

Tactics to Overcome
- Tactics to Overcome: To address the first challenge, include a mix of easy and challenging questions in your trivia game to cater to all family members' knowledge levels. To tackle the second challenge, rotate themes and categories periodically to keep the game fresh and exciting. Encourage healthy competition among family members to maintain their interest.

TIP 31: DIY CUSTOM OUTER SHELLS

Category
Home Assistants

Brief
Personalize the physical appearance of your home assistant by crafting custom outer shells or covers. Match them with your home decor or themes.

Steps
1. Choose the material for your custom shell (e.g., wood, fabric, or 3D-printed).
2. Measure your home assistant's dimensions.
3. Design or choose a pattern for your shell.
4. Craft or assemble the custom shell. 5. Place it over your home assistant.

Practical Challenges
- Practical Challenges: One challenge is ensuring that the custom shell fits the home assistant properly. Another challenge is keeping the shell clean and free from dust or damage.

Tactics to Overcome
- Tactics to Overcome: To address the first challenge, double-check your measurements and design before crafting the shell. Consider professional assistance for precise fitting if needed. To tackle the second challenge, periodically clean the custom shell and ensure it's made from materials that are easy to maintain. Avoid exposing it to excessive moisture or direct sunlight.

CHAPTER 5 - GAMING CONSOLE CUSTOMIZATION

TIP 32: HYDRO-DIP CONTROLLER SKINS

Category
Personalized controller skins

Brief
Hydro-dipping is a water transfer painting process. This technique gives your controllers a unique, vibrant look. It's not only a way to personalize but also offers a protective layer against scratches. Use it to reflect your personality, or simply to distinguish controllers within a household. Positive impacts include added aesthetic appeal and improved grip.

Steps
1. Disassemble the controller.
2. Clean and primer the parts.
3. Fill a container with water.
4. Spray paints of choice on the water surface. 5. Dip the controller parts into the water. 6. Allow to dry and reassemble.

Practical Challenges
Disassembly might void warranty. Paint might not adhere properly if steps aren't followed precisely.

Tactics to Overcome
Ensure the controller is clean. Use a primer. Be cautious with the amount of paint used; too much can cause clumping.

TIP 33: AMBIENT LED CONSOLE LIGHTING

Category
Unique LED light mods for consoles

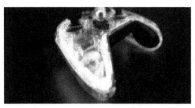

Brief
Add an ambient glow to your console using LED strip lights. It elevates the look of the gaming area, making gaming sessions more immersive. Great for late-night sessions, reducing eye strain and adding to the ambiance of the room.

Steps
1. Measure console's perimeter.
2. Purchase the correct length of LED strip lights.
3. Attach LED strips using adhesive back.
4. Connect to a power source. 5. Use remote to adjust colors and patterns.

Practical Challenges
LED might overheat if left on for prolonged periods. Some consoles might not have space for LED attachments.

Tactics to Overcome
Opt for LEDs designed for consoles. Place in a well-ventilated area. Turn off when not in use.

TIP 34: DIY MULTI-CONSOLE CHARGING DOCK

Category
DIY charging station designs

Brief
Building a multi-console charging dock organizes and streamlines your gaming area. Eliminate cable clutter, charge multiple devices, and enhance room aesthetics. It's beneficial for gamers with multiple devices seeking a centralized charging hub.

Steps
1. Measure space required for all devices.
2. Sketch a design with allocated slots.
3. Gather materials like wood, paint, and a multi-port USB hub.
4. Cut and assemble the dock. 5. Paint and finish as desired.

Practical Challenges
Incorrect measurements might lead to unfit slots. Overcharging can damage devices.

Tactics to Overcome
Measure multiple times before cutting. Use a surge-protected power source. Add labels for each slot.

TIP 35: CUSTOM IN-GAME BANNER CREATION

Category
Custom in-game banners and icons

Brief
Reflect your identity in multiplayer games using custom banners. It makes your profile recognizable in the gaming community, and displays your style and creativity. Especially valuable for streamers or online influencers to brand their presence.

Steps
1. Design a banner using graphic software.
2. Ensure dimensions fit the game's requirements.
3. Save in a compatible format.
4. Upload in the game's customization settings.

Practical Challenges
Some games may have content restrictions. Design might not look as envisioned in-game.

Tactics to Overcome
Keep designs simple and clear. Review game's content guidelines. Use high-resolution images.

TIP 36: GAME SORTING TACTICS

Category
Tailored game sorting for quick access

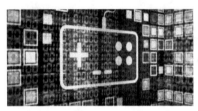

Brief
Digital game libraries can get cluttered. Sorting games by frequency of use or genre enhances accessibility. For gamers with large libraries, this saves time and streamlines the gaming experience.

Steps
1. Navigate to the game library.
2. Use filters or folders.
3. Organize games based on preference.
4. Save settings.

Practical Challenges
Not all platforms offer robust sorting options. Might have to re-sort after updates.

Tactics to Overcome
Regularly check and update your sorting. Backup game data before making significant changes.

TIP 37: CUSTOM CONSOLE BOOT SOUNDS

Category
Exclusive startup sounds

Brief
Customize the auditory experience every time you turn on your console. It personalizes the device and can serve as a fun, auditory marker that gaming time has started.

Steps
1. Access console settings.
2. Navigate to sound preferences.
3. Upload your custom sound (check format compatibility).
4. Set as default boot sound.

Practical Challenges
Some consoles might not support this feature. Sound might be distorted if not optimized.

Tactics to Overcome
Ensure sound quality is high. Test multiple times before finalizing. Keep backups of default settings.

TIP 38: CREATE DIGITAL ACHIEVEMENT BADGES

Category
Personalized game achievements

Brief
Digital badges are a visual representation of achievements. Create custom badges for personal milestones. Adds a layer of personal challenge and fulfillment to games.

Steps
1. Design badge using graphic software.
2. Save in compatible format.
3. Use game modding tools to integrate custom badges.

Practical Challenges
May conflict with game updates. Some games might detect this as a modification.

Tactics to Overcome
Always backup game data. Use badges for personal satisfaction, not public validation.

TIP 39: THEMED CONSOLE DUST COVERS

Category
Crafted dust covers with themed designs

Brief
Dust covers protect consoles while adding aesthetic appeal. Using themed designs can showcase your favorite game or series. A practical and decorative solution for gamers.

Steps
1. Measure console dimensions.
2. Select a theme and design.
3. Choose material (e.g., cloth).
4. Cut and sew the cover. 5. Add decorative elements.

Practical Challenges
Improper sizing might restrict ventilation. Might not fit with attached cables or peripherals.

Tactics to Overcome
Ensure cover is breathable. Design with openings for cables. Regularly wash or dust off.

CHAPTER 6 - EARBUDS AND HEADPHONES MAKEOVER

TIP 40: CUSTOM MOLDED EAR TIPS

Category
Crafting Custom Ear Tips

Brief
Custom molded ear tips provide a unique and secure fit for earbuds, enhancing the audio experience. This trick ensures your earbuds stay in place during activities like running or gym workouts. By crafting a personalized mold, users can experience enhanced bass and reduced ambient noise. For daily commuters or fitness enthusiasts, this ensures better sound isolation and comfort.

Steps
1. Buy a silicone ear kit.
2. Follow the instructions to make an impression of your ear.
3. Let it dry and attach to earbuds.

Practical Challenges
Achieving the perfect mold can be tricky. Over-molding can cause discomfort, while under-molding might not hold earbuds securely.

Tactics to Overcome
1. Watch tutorial videos before starting.
2. Test the mold's fit before finalizing.
3. Adjust and reshape as necessary.

TIP 41: DIY WOODEN HEADPHONE STAND

Category
Personalized Headphone Stands

Brief
A personalized headphone stand not only keeps your headphones organized but also becomes a statement piece on your desk. It represents one's style and preference. For anyone who loves DIY projects or wishes for a clutter-free workspace, this trick provides a unique and functional solution.

Steps
1. Choose a wooden plank.
2. Sketch the desired shape.
3. Saw carefully along the sketch.
4. Sand to smooth edges. 5. Varnish or paint as desired.

Practical Challenges
The wood might splinter during sawing, and achieving a professional finish can be challenging.

Tactics to Overcome
1. Use fine-grit sandpaper for smoothness.
2. Apply multiple thin coats of varnish.
3. Always saw with the grain.

TIP 42: BEADED WIRE WRAPS

Category
Unique Wire-Wrapping Techniques

Brief

Beaded wire wraps for headphones not only prevent tangling but also give a unique, aesthetic look to otherwise plain wires. For those tired of untangling wires or seeking a stylish accessory, this trick serves both purposes. It turns ordinary headphones into a trendy, personalized item.

Steps
1. Choose beads of preferred colors and sizes.
2. Start threading beads onto the wire.
3. Secure after every few beads.
4. Continue until the desired length is covered.

Practical Challenges
Beads can slide off if not secured properly. The weight of beads might slightly affect the headphone's comfort.

Tactics to Overcome
1. Use clear elastic bands to secure beads in intervals.
2. Opt for lighter, smaller beads.
3. Don't overcrowd; leave some wire spaces.

TIP 43: GENRE-SPECIFIC EQ SETTINGS

Category
Tailored EQ Settings

Brief
Different music genres have distinct sonic elements. Tailoring EQ settings enhances the listening experience. This trick is essential for audiophiles or anyone passionate about music. For daily listeners, it ensures that every track sounds its best, enhancing the overall experience.

Steps
1. Open the device's sound settings.
2. Adjust the EQ bars based on the genre. (E.g., Boost bass for hip-hop, enhance mids for rock.)
3. Save custom presets for each genre.

Practical Challenges
Adjusting the EQ might distort some tracks if not done correctly. It can be time-consuming to find the perfect settings.

Tactics to Overcome
1. Research genre-specific EQ presets online.
2. Start with slight adjustments.
3. Always test with multiple tracks before finalizing.

TIP 44: HAND-STITCHED CARRYING POUCH

Category
Exclusive Carrying Pouch Designs

Brief
A hand-stitched carrying pouch protects earbuds and showcases individual style. For those wanting a unique storage solution or concerned about wear and tear, this trick offers protection with a personal touch. Handmade items always have sentimental value, making daily use special.

Steps
1. Choose a fabric.
2. Sketch the pouch size on it.
3. Cut out the design.
4. Stitch the edges, leaving the top open. 5. Add buttons or zippers if desired.

Practical Challenges
Stitching can be uneven, affecting the pouch's durability. Choosing the wrong fabric might not protect the earbuds sufficiently.

Tactics to Overcome
1. Opt for durable fabric like denim.
2. Double-stitch the edges for strength.
3. Use padding inside for extra protection.

TIP 45: DIY HEADPHONE DECALS

Category
DIY Custom Decals and Stickers

Brief
Decals are a fun way to customize headphones. This trick allows users to showcase their preferences or hobbies. For daily users, it adds a flair to their gear, making it easily recognizable and uniquely theirs.

Steps
1. Buy printable sticker sheets.
2. Design or download images.
3. Print the designs.
4. Cut them out carefully. 5. Stick onto the headphones.

Practical Challenges
Decals might wear off with time. Wrong placement can affect the headphone's functionality.

Tactics to Overcome
1. Apply a clear sealant over stickers for longevity.
2. Ensure stickers don't cover any vents or ports.
3. Choose high-quality sticker paper.

TIP 46: CUSTOM VOICE PROMPTS

Category
Personalized Voice Prompts

Brief
Custom voice prompts add a personal touch to headphones, especially those with built-in AI. This trick makes tech feel more personal. For daily users, it can be a fun reminder of a loved one's voice or a favorite quote, enhancing the user experience.

Steps
1. Record the desired voice prompt.
2. Connect headphones to a computer.
3. Use the manufacturer's software to replace default prompts.

Practical Challenges
Some headphones might not support custom prompts. The recorded quality might differ from the original sound.

Tactics to Overcome
1. Use high-quality mics for recording.
2. Ensure compatibility before purchase.
3. Edit and enhance voice recordings for clarity.

TIP 47: VINTAGE COILED CABLES

Category
Crafting Coiled Cables

Brief
Coiled cables bring back the vintage vibe while providing elasticity. For daily users who appreciate the retro look or seek a functional solution to cable length, this trick adds style while ensuring mobility.

Steps
1. Wrap the headphone cable around a rod tightly.
2. Apply heat using a hairdryer until the cable holds the shape.
3. Let it cool and remove from the rod.

Practical Challenges
Applying too much heat can damage the cable. Achieving the desired coil tightness can be tricky.

Tactics to Overcome
1. Monitor the heating process closely.
2. Practice with a disposable cable first.
3. Adjust the rod size based on desired coil size.

CHAPTER 7 - E-READER PERSONALIZATION TACTICS

TIP 48: CUSTOM SCREENSAVERS

Category
E-Reader Personalization

Brief
Customizing your e-reader with personal photos adds a touch of individuality to your device, making the reading experience even more personal. It often serves as a motivation to read more. In daily life, every time you unlock your device, memories or a photo of a loved one could greet you, enhancing emotional well-being.

Steps
1. Select a high-resolution photo.
2. Convert to grayscale if e-reader is black and white.
3. Use editing tools to adjust the size to fit your screen.
4. Upload to e-reader.

Practical Challenges
It's not always easy finding high-resolution photos that look good in black and white or grayscale. The photo's dimensions might also not align with the e-reader's screen.

Tactics to Overcome
Select photos with fewer details. Convert images to grayscale and test their appearance. Ensure dimensions match or crop them. Use tools like Canva for resizing.

TIP 49: HANDCRAFTED PROTECTIVE COVERS

Category
E-Reader Personalization

Brief
A protective cover not only shields your e-reader from potential damages but can also showcase your personality. By crafting it yourself, you can select materials that resonate with your style. In daily scenarios like commuting, a unique cover can be a conversation starter and also make locating your device easier among other gadgets.

Steps
1. Measure e-reader dimensions.
2. Choose a durable material.
3. Cut, stitch, and decorate as desired.

Practical Challenges
Crafting can be time-consuming. Getting the right fit or choosing a material that lasts can be challenging.

Tactics to Overcome
To reduce time, consider semi-DIY options like buying a plain cover and personalizing it. Ensure measurements are accurate. Seek materials known for durability.

TIP 50: PERSONALIZED FONT IMPORTS

Category
E-Reader Personalization

Brief
E-readers often come with standard fonts, but importing personalized fonts can dramatically enhance reading comfort and aesthetics. Whether for visual impairments or just personal style, custom fonts make daily reading sessions enjoyable and strain-free.

Steps
1. Find a compatible font.
2. Download and save it.
3. Transfer to e-reader using a USB cable.
4. Select the new font from settings.

Practical Challenges
Compatibility issues might arise. Overloading with numerous fonts can reduce device performance.

Tactics to Overcome
Limit the number of fonts you import. Ensure compatibility by checking e-reader specifications. Backup before making changes.

TIP 51: UNIQUE HIGHLIGHT COLORS AND NOTE-TAKING STYLES

Category
E-Reader Personalization

Brief
Personalizing highlight colors and note-taking styles can make revisiting noted sections easier and more intuitive. In daily reading, particularly for academic or research purposes, such customizations can streamline revisions and improve retention.

Steps
1. Access e-reader settings.
2. Navigate to highlighting and notes.
3. Choose desired colors/styles.

Practical Challenges
Not all e-readers allow color customizations. Adjusting to new styles can be initially confusing.

Tactics to Overcome
Stick to a few colors/styles for consistency. Use color legends if needed. Check device specifications for customization possibilities.

TIP 52: TAILORED READING GOALS AND REWARDS

Category
E-Reader Personalization

Brief
Setting tailored reading goals with personalized rewards can boost motivation. In our daily lives, where distractions are rife, a system of rewards can provide an incentive to commit to reading, ensuring personal growth and relaxation.

Steps
1. Set a realistic monthly reading target.
2. Choose a reward upon completion.
3. Monitor progress daily.

Practical Challenges
Sticking to goals can be challenging. Daily disruptions can hinder progress. The chosen reward might not motivate sufficiently over time.

Tactics to Overcome
Periodically review and adjust goals. Ensure rewards are genuinely enticing. Integrate reading into daily routines, like before bedtime.

TIP 53: DIY STYLUS HOLDERS

Category
E-Reader Personalization

Brief
E-readers with touchscreen capabilities often come with or support styluses. A DIY stylus holder ensures that the stylus is always nearby, preventing loss. In daily usage, especially during commutes or travel, having the stylus accessible can enhance user experience.

Steps
1. Measure stylus dimensions.
2. Select materials (elastic bands, leather).
3. Craft and attach to e-reader cover.

Practical Challenges
Crafting the right fit can be tricky. Improper attachment can damage the e-reader cover.

Tactics to Overcome
Use adjustable materials like elastic. Attach using non-permanent methods first to test position and fit.

TIP 54: EXCLUSIVE BACKGROUND THEMES

Category
E-Reader Personalization

Brief
Exclusive background themes personalize the aesthetics of your e-reader, making the device feel truly yours. Daily interactions with the device become more enjoyable, positively impacting the reading experience.

Steps
1. Browse and select a desired theme or create one.
2. Download and transfer to e-reader.
3. Set as the default background from settings.

Practical Challenges
Theme might not display correctly on all screens. Overloading with numerous themes can affect performance.

Tactics to Overcome
Test themes before settling. Limit the number of themes. Ensure they're optimized for e-reader resolution.

TIP 55: PERSONAL BOOK CATEGORIZATION HACKS

Category
E-Reader Personalization

Brief
Instead of default genre-based categorizations, personal hacks like 'To be read on a rainy day' can make book selection more intuitive. In daily life, when mood-based reading preferences change, such categories can enhance the reading experience.

Steps
1. Analyze reading habits and moods.
2. Create categories accordingly.
3. Sort books into these personal categories.

Practical Challenges
Initial sorting can be time-consuming. Some e-readers might not support custom categories.

Tactics to Overcome
Take a phased approach to sorting. Prioritize frequently read books. Check device specifications for categorization possibilities.

CHAPTER 8 - SMART TV AND STREAMING DEVICE HACKS

TIP 56: CUSTOM BACKDROP SELECTION

Category
Ambient Backdrop

Brief
Customizing the backdrop of your Smart TV can provide a personalized touch to your living space. It's especially useful for those who value aesthetics and want their TV to fit seamlessly into their room's theme. You can use photos from a recent family trip, favorite artworks, or nature scenes to help set a mood. It uplifts the visual appeal and can trigger positive memories every time the TV is turned on.

Steps
- Access settings of your Smart TV.
- Navigate to display settings.
- Choose the option to change the backdrop.
- Upload your chosen image.
- Adjust scale and positioning as required.

Practical Challenges
Setting up a custom backdrop can sometimes lead to lower image resolution or incorrect image scaling, making the image look distorted. Using a landscape image for a portrait-oriented space or vice versa can also cause issues.

Tactics to Overcome
Always choose high-resolution images. Understand the aspect ratio of your TV screen and choose or crop images accordingly. Testing multiple images will allow you to select the one that aligns best.

TIP 57: DIY REMOTE HOLDER

Category
Remote Control

Brief
Every living room has faced the perennial problem of the lost remote. Creating a handcrafted remote control holder not only ensures its safekeeping but also adds a personal touch to the room's décor. It's an eco-friendly way to upcycle household materials and ensures that the remote is always within reach, enhancing daily convenience.

Steps
• Choose a material (e.g., an old shoebox, wood plank).
• Measure remote dimensions.
• Create slots or spaces for remote.
• Decorate as desired.
• Place in an easily accessible location.

Practical Challenges
While DIY projects can be fun, they can sometimes end up being less durable than store-bought items. There's also a risk of the remote not fitting properly if measurements are inaccurate.

Tactics to Overcome
Use durable materials for the base structure. Ensure measurements are taken with a little allowance for easy placement and removal. Consider layering the interior with soft fabric to prevent scratches.

TIP 58: UNIQUE AVATAR PROFILES

Category
User Profile

Brief
Personalized user profiles with unique avatars can provide a quick identification for multiple users of a single Smart TV or streaming device. It's especially beneficial for families. It not only makes the TV experience personal but also keeps watch histories and recommendations distinct for each user.

Steps
• Navigate to user profile settings on your device.
• Choose the option to edit or change avatar.
• Select from available choices or upload a personal picture.
• Save settings.

Practical Challenges
With multiple users, there can be a challenge in managing and differentiating profiles. Inadvertent changes to the wrong profile can disrupt personalized recommendations.

Tactics to Overcome
Regularly review and update profiles. Educate all users on the importance of selecting their own profile before using the TV or device. A password or PIN for each profile can also prevent inadvertent switches.

TIP 59: FAMILY VIDEO SCREENSAVERS

Category
Screensaver

Brief
Converting family videos into screensavers for your TV can be a delightful way to relive memories. It adds a personal touch and can serve as a conversation starter with guests. It reminds us of precious moments and makes the TV more than just an entertainment device.

Steps
• Convert family video to a compatible format.
• Transfer to your TV or streaming device.
• Access display settings.
• Set the video as screensaver.

Practical Challenges
Some videos may not be compatible or could appear pixelated when enlarged. Long videos might also consume more power when used as screensavers.

Tactics to Overcome
Choose videos that have been shot in good quality. Trim videos to shorter lengths to use them as screensavers to ensure they loop seamlessly and use less power.

TIP 60: QUICK ACCESS APP ARRANGEMENT

Category
App Arrangement

Brief
An organized app layout ensures you can quickly access frequently used apps, enhancing efficiency. A clutter-free screen can also reduce cognitive load, making selections quicker and reducing decision fatigue. Especially on days when you want to quickly jump to your favorite show after a long day.

Steps
• Access the app arrangement settings on your device.
• Organize apps based on frequency of use.
• Group similar apps together.
• Remove or hide unused apps.

Practical Challenges
Over time, with new apps being added or old ones becoming obsolete, the arrangement can become cluttered, requiring regular maintenance.

Tactics to Overcome
Set a bi-monthly or quarterly reminder to review and reorganize apps. This ensures the layout remains efficient and user-friendly.

TIP 61: CUSTOM LED SOUNDBARS

Category
Audio Customization

Brief
Adding LEDs to your soundbar enhances the audio-visual experience, especially during evening movie nights. It can sync with the audio, pulsating to the rhythm, adding an immersive feel. This not only elevates the entertainment experience but can also serve as ambient lighting for the room.

Steps
• Purchase an LED strip with adhesive backing.
• Attach the LED strip to the back of the soundbar.
• Connect it to a power source.
• Sync with the audio output if the feature is available.

Practical Challenges
LED strips can sometimes detach due to heat from the soundbar. The color or rhythm synchronization might not always be accurate.

Tactics to Overcome
Opt for high-quality LED strips designed for electronics. Ensure there's ample space for ventilation. Consider investing in soundbars with built-in LED customization features.

TIP 62: TAILORED MOVIE SUGGESTIONS

Category
Recommendation Settings

Brief
Personalized movie recommendations can enhance viewing experiences, ensuring you spend more time enjoying content than searching for it. By tailoring recommendations, you're provided with content that aligns with your preferences, mood, and viewing habits.

Steps
• Access the content platform's settings.
• Navigate to recommendation or preference settings.
• Rate watched movies or shows.
• Set genre preferences.
• Regularly update viewing habits.

Practical Challenges
Over-reliance on algorithms can sometimes lead to repetitive content suggestions or missing out on new genres.

Tactics to Overcome
Diversify your watchlist occasionally to give the algorithm a broader dataset. Explore editor's picks or trending sections to discover fresh content.

TIP 63: VOICE COMMANDS FOR SHOWS

Category
Voice Command

Brief
In today's era of vast content, voice commands streamline the process of accessing your favorite shows. Just a quick voice prompt can swiftly take you to the desired content, eliminating the need to navigate through menus, thus saving time.

Steps
• Ensure your device supports voice commands.
• Press the voice command button on the remote.
• Clearly state the desired show, app, or function.
• Let the device process and execute the command.

Practical Challenges
Ambient noise can sometimes hinder accurate voice recognition. Multiple similar sounding titles can also confuse the device.

Tactics to Overcome
Speak clearly and distinctly. Reduce ambient noise when using the feature. If there are recognition issues, consider using specific phrases or names for better accuracy.

CHAPTER 9 - SMART HOME DEVICE TWEAKS

TIP 64: PERSONALIZED SMART LIGHTING MOODS

Category
Smart Lighting

Brief
Creating personalized lighting moods can drastically transform the ambience of a room. Different lighting settings can be used to evoke specific feelings or moods. For example, a warm yellow light can replicate a cozy evening. These customized settings can be used during dinner, movie nights, or reading sessions, providing an enhanced living experience. It positively affects our mood, providing comfort and personalization to daily life.

Steps
1. Choose a smart lighting system compatible with customization.
2. Use the app to adjust colors and brightness.
3. Save presets for different moods.
4. Test in different room settings.

Practical Challenges
Getting the perfect mood setting might require multiple adjustments. It can be challenging to choose colors that are both functional and evocative. There's a story of someone who set a "party" mode too bright, turning a fun evening into a glaring experience.

Tactics to Overcome
1. Start with pre-made templates before customization.
2. Check effects in real-time, adjusting accordingly. Remember, the party story serves as a lesson: practical functionality is just as crucial as aesthetics.

TIP 65: CUSTOM DOORBELL TUNES

Category
Doorbell Chimes

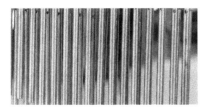

Brief
Customizing your doorbell tune can make homecoming a unique experience. It allows homeowners to select a sound that resonates with their personal style or mood. This tweak becomes handy during festive seasons, allowing homes to stand out. It provides a personal touch to a usually mundane aspect of our homes and can often bring joy or a chuckle to visitors.

Steps
1. Buy a programmable doorbell.
2. Upload desired tune or sound.
3. Adjust the volume.
4. Test the sound before finalizing.

Practical Challenges
The challenge is finding a tune that's distinct yet not too disruptive or annoying after repeated plays. Some have shared tales of choosing elaborate tunes that eventually became irksome.

Tactics to Overcome
Stick to melodies that are short and sweet. It might be fun to change it up monthly or seasonally to keep it fresh. Use holidays or special occasions as reminders to switch tunes.

TIP 66: DECORATIVE MOUNTS FOR SMART DEVICES

Category
Smart Device Decoration

Brief
Smart devices are functional but can sometimes clash with home aesthetics. Creating decorative mounts helps blend these devices into the home decor or even make them stand out as a feature. This ensures that while benefiting from the tech, homeowners can still maintain their home's aesthetic feel.

Steps
1. Measure the device dimensions.
2. Choose a theme/style that matches home decor.
3. Craft or purchase the decorative mount.
4. Install the device within the mount.

Practical Challenges
An initial challenge is ensuring the decor doesn't interfere with the device's functionality. For instance, a decorative mount might hinder a camera's view or muffle a speaker's sound.

Tactics to Overcome
Ensure the mount has openings where necessary, like for a camera lens or speaker. Test the device thoroughly after installing in the mount to ensure optimal functionality.

TIP 67: LED NOTIFICATION SEQUENCES

Category
Smart Notifications

Brief
LED sequences for notifications provide immediate visual feedback about an event without being intrusive. For instance, a pulsing blue light might indicate it's raining outside. This provides a silent yet effective way to stay informed about various events or notifications. It can be particularly useful in scenarios where silence is golden, like when a baby is sleeping.

Steps
1. Identify the events you want notifications for.
2. Choose a distinct LED sequence for each.
3. Program the sequences using the device's app.
4. Test to ensure correct functioning.

Practical Challenges
It can be challenging to remember each sequence. Overloading with many sequences can lead to confusion. A new parent once had so many sequences that they misinterpreted one and mistakenly thought their baby's room was too cold.

Tactics to Overcome
Keep the number of sequences limited and intuitive. Maintain a written log until they're committed to memory. Periodically review and adjust as needed.

TIP 68: FAMILY TRIVIA ON HOME ASSISTANTS

Category
Interactive Family Games

Brief
Using smart home assistants for family trivia games creates bonding opportunities. These can be personalized to family memories, ensuring laughter and nostalgia. It's a great way to revisit shared memories and even educate younger family members about their history.

Steps
1. Collate a list of family trivia questions.
2. Input these into the smart home assistant.
3. Set up a command to initiate the trivia game.
4. Gather family and enjoy!

Practical Challenges
The challenge is keeping the trivia updated and relevant. A family once used the same trivia for so long that newer family members felt left out since they weren't part of the older memories.

Tactics to Overcome
Regularly update trivia, especially after significant family events. Ensure questions span across different time frames and include recent memories.

TIP 69: TAILORED SMART MIRROR MOOD LIGHTING

Category
Smart Mirror Customization

Brief
Smart mirrors aren't just reflective surfaces; they're interactive devices. Tailoring their lighting can enhance experiences, from a soft glow for makeup application to bright light for detailed tasks. The right light can set the day's tone, ensuring you start on a positive note.

Steps
1. Choose a smart mirror with customizable lighting.
2. Adjust light settings for specific tasks.
3. Save presets.
4. Use accordingly.

Practical Challenges
Adjusting to the right brightness or hue can be tricky. Too bright, and it's blinding; too dim, and tasks become difficult. A user once shared about setting the light too dim for makeup, resulting in a makeup disaster at an event.

Tactics to Overcome
Regularly adjust and test in various scenarios. For makeup, ensure the light closely replicates your destination's lighting (e.g., office, party).

TIP 70: DIY DECORATIVE STICKERS FOR APPLIANCES

Category
Appliance Personalization

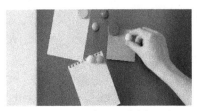

Brief
Appliances are functional but often generic. DIY decorative stickers add a personal touch, making homes feel unique. For instance, turning a fridge into a family photo album or adding floral themes to a washing machine can transform a space.

Steps
1. Decide on a theme.
2. Source or create stickers.
3. Clean the appliance surface.
4. Carefully apply stickers. 5. Seal with a protective layer if necessary.

Practical Challenges
Over time, stickers can peel or fade. An individual recounted their disappointment when their painstakingly applied stickers began to peel within a month.

Tactics to Overcome
Opt for high-quality stickers. Ensure the appliance surface is clean and free from grease before applying. Consider using a sealant for added protection.

TIP 71: VOICE-CONTROLLED APPLIANCE MODES

Category
Voice Control Enhancement

Brief
Making appliances respond to voice commands elevates convenience. Instead of manually adjusting, simply command your coffee maker or oven. This allows for hands-free operation, which can be particularly useful when multitasking.

Steps
1. Ensure appliances are voice-command compatible.
2. Configure voice commands through the corresponding app.
3. Train the device to recognize your voice.
4. Use voice commands to control appliances.

Practical Challenges
Voice recognition isn't always perfect. Some users have shared stories of their appliances misinterpreting commands, leading to unexpected results.

Tactics to Overcome
Regularly train the voice recognition system. Use clear, distinct commands. Ensure the device's firmware is always updated for optimal performance.

CHAPTER 10 - CAMERA AND PHOTOGRAPHY GEAR ENHANCEMENTS

TIP 72: CRAFTING CUSTOM CAMERA STRAPS

Category
Camera Gear Customization

Brief
Personalized camera straps provide not just aesthetic appeal but also comfort tailored to the user. Having a unique strap sets one apart, while also ensuring the weight distribution of the camera suits the wearer's needs. Whether you're a professional photographer or just someone taking snapshots, these straps ensure easy access and reduce fatigue, enhancing daily photography experiences.

Steps
1. Measure the desired strap length.
2. Choose material (leather, cloth).
3. Add cushioning for shoulder comfort.
4. Embroider or print a design. 5. Attach the strap ends to the camera.

Practical Challenges
Oftentimes, users might pick materials that wear out quickly or dyes that fade. An inappropriate length might also hinder easy camera accessibility.

Tactics to Overcome
When selecting materials, prioritize durability. Test colors for fade resistance. Regularly inspect the strap's condition, especially attachment points. Consider ergonomics to decide the strap's width and padding.

TIP 73: DIY PROTECTIVE CASING FOR RUGGED SHOOTS

Category
Protective Camera Gear

Brief
Outdoor or extreme environment shoots can expose cameras to potential damage. A DIY protective casing can shield against dirt, moisture, and minor shocks, ensuring the equipment's longevity. This trick benefits those who often engage in adventure photography or shoot in unpredictable environments. It directly impacts the durability and lifespan of the camera, thus securing your investment.

Steps
1. Measure camera dimensions.
2. Choose a waterproof, shock-resistant material.
3. Cut and shape the material to fit the camera.
4. Ensure accessibility to camera controls. 5. Test in controlled rugged conditions.

Practical Challenges
Crafting a case that's both protective and functional can be challenging. Over-protection might restrict quick access to controls or limit articulation of movable parts.

Tactics to Overcome
Ensure a balance between protection and functionality. Periodically check for wear and tear. Prioritize vulnerable parts like the lens and back screen. Consider adding protective filters to the lens.

TIP 74: CUSTOM FLASH DIFFUSERS USING HOUSEHOLD ITEMS

Category
DIY Photography Enhancements

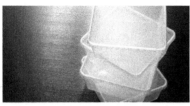

Brief
Flash photography can sometimes be harsh. Custom flash diffusers soften the light, producing natural, flattering results. Instead of buying professional diffusers, household items like white plastic containers or fabric can be used. This trick is essential for indoor photography, especially when bouncing light isn't an option. It transforms flash-lit photos from looking artificial to professional.

Steps
1. Choose a translucent material.
2. Shape it to fit the flash head.
3. Secure it without obstructing the flash.
4. Test by taking photos with and without the diffuser.

Practical Challenges
A wrongly chosen material might alter the color temperature or block too much light. Also, some DIY diffusers might look unprofessional in formal settings.

Tactics to Overcome
Choose neutral-colored materials. Test different materials for desired softness. For formal gigs, refine the diffuser's appearance or have a professional-looking backup.

TIP 75: PERSONALIZED WATERMARK TEMPLATES

Category
Photo Branding

Brief
Watermarks not only deter unauthorized usage of photos but also brand your work. A personalized watermark reflects one's style and makes photos instantly recognizable. Every photographer, amateur or professional, should consider this trick to protect and brand their art. It makes one's work stand out and ensures that even shared photos carry the creator's signature.

Steps
1. Design a unique yet subtle logo.
2. Choose a placement that doesn't distract from the photo.
3. Use photo editing software to create a watermark template.
4. Apply to photos as needed.

Practical Challenges
Overly bold watermarks can distract from the photo. Placing them incorrectly might make them easy to crop out.

Tactics to Overcome
Design a watermark that is noticeable but not overpowering. Consider using semi-transparent watermarks. Place them in a position where cropping would harm the photo's composition.

TIP 76: PERSONALIZED LENS CAP DESIGNS

Category
Camera Gear Personalization

Brief
Lens caps, while practical, are typically generic. Personalizing them not only adds an aesthetic flair but can also be functional, for instance, by labeling them for different lenses. This ensures quicker lens swaps, especially for photographers with extensive gear. It serves as both an organization hack and a style statement, refining the photography process.

Steps
1. Choose a lens cap that fits securely.
2. Clean the surface for better adherence.
3. Paint or add decals.
4. Label for specific lenses if desired.

Practical Challenges
Paint or decals might wear off over time. Over-decorating can make the cap cumbersome to use or not fit well.

Tactics to Overcome
Use durable paints or stickers meant for plastics. Keep designs simple to ensure cap functionality isn't compromised. Use clear protective sprays to seal designs.

TIP 77: TAILORED ON-CAMERA SETTINGS FOR SPECIFIC STYLES

Category
Camera Setting Optimization

Brief
Every photographer has a style, and optimizing camera settings to match this can save post-processing time. Whether one leans towards high contrast urban shots or soft-focus nature imagery, tailoring settings aids in capturing the desired look right from the click. This trick is indispensable for those wanting to minimize editing and get consistent shots.

Steps
1. Identify the style you lean towards.
2. Adjust camera settings like contrast, saturation, and sharpness accordingly.
3. Save these as custom profiles for easy access.
4. Test and refine based on results.

Practical Challenges
Adjusting settings might be complex on some cameras. Over-customization can sometimes limit versatility in unforeseen shooting scenarios.

Tactics to Overcome
Familiarize oneself with the camera manual. Start with small tweaks, gradually refining them. Consider having multiple profiles for different shooting scenarios.

TIP 78: EXCLUSIVE PHOTO STORAGE ORGANIZATION HACKS

Category
Photo Management

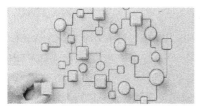

Brief
As photography collections grow, organizing them becomes paramount. A structured storage system ensures quicker access, better backups, and streamlined editing processes. This trick is vital for any avid photographer, reducing time wasted searching for specific photos and ensuring a smooth workflow from shoot to post-processing.

Steps
1. Sort photos by date, location, or theme.
2. Use consistent naming conventions.
3. Back up in at least two separate locations.
4. Regularly review and declutter.

Practical Challenges
Over time, storage can become cluttered. Backup systems might fail. Searching for specific photos in large collections can become time-consuming.

Tactics to Overcome
Adopt a strict routine for transferring and organizing photos post-shoot. Use reliable backup solutions, including cloud storage. Employ metadata tags for even more detailed searching.

TIP 79: HANDCRAFTED TRIPOD ACCESSORIES

Category
DIY Photography Enhancements

Brief
Tripods, though highly functional, can be enhanced with handcrafted accessories. From added hooks for stabilization to custom grips for better handling, these tweaks ensure stability and ease of use. It benefits photographers who often shoot in varied conditions, ensuring their tripod isn't just another tool but a tailored extension of their craft.

Steps
1. Identify areas of improvement on the tripod.
2. For stability, add hooks at the bottom to hang weights.
3. Craft cushioned grips for comfort.
4. Attach DIY holders for additional gear like reflectors.

Practical Challenges
DIY additions might alter the tripod's balance. Overloading with accessories can affect its portability and setup speed.

Tactics to Overcome
Always test the tripod's stability post any modification. Avoid permanent alterations; instead, use detachable enhancements. Keep a checklist to ensure quick setups even with added accessories.

CHAPTER 11 - PERSONALIZING DRONES AND ROBOTICS

TIP 80: CREATIVE DRONE SKINNING

Category
DIY Personalization

Brief
Drones, while robust, often come in standard colors. Skinning them allows for individuality, easier spotting in the sky, and protection from minor scratches. A well-designed skin can set your drone apart, make it easier to identify in case of loss, and reflects the user's style. It elevates the droning experience from a mere hobby to a personalized statement.

Steps
1. Choose a high-quality vinyl wrap.
2. Clean the drone's surface.
3. Apply the wrap carefully, smoothing out bubbles.
4. Trim excess material.

Practical Challenges
Skinning may affect drone sensors or add weight. The wrap might peel in high-speeds or challenging weather. An example scenario is a drone enthusiast finding the skin peeling off after flights due to not smoothing out air bubbles properly.

Tactics to Overcome
Opt for lightweight, high-quality wraps. Ensure skins don't cover sensors. Regularly inspect and maintain the skin, especially post-flights. Smoothing tools can help in proper application.

TIP 81: CINEMATIC FLIGHT PRESETS

Category
Drone Flight Customization

Brief
Default drone flight modes may not capture cinematic shots effectively. Creating custom flight paths and speed settings can elevate video quality. In daily use, such presets save time, allowing for on-the-go filming, especially during golden hours, weddings, or dynamic sports. It provides professional-grade footage without the hassle.

Steps
1. Study classic cinematic shots.
2. Adjust drone speed and angles to mimic these.
3. Save these custom paths.
4. Practice flying in these modes.

Practical Challenges
Presets might not work in all scenarios. Unexpected obstacles or wind can alter paths. For instance, a preset meant for forest filming might be challenging in an urban setting due to buildings.

Tactics to Overcome
Use obstacle avoidance features. Monitor real-time feedback and adjust as needed. Having multiple presets for different environments can ensure versatility.

TIP 82: VOICE-CONTROLLED ROBOTICS

Category
Voice Control Customization

Brief
In an age of automation, voice controlling your robotic devices like vacuum cleaners or automated assistants brings convenience. Imagine verbally setting up your robotic vacuum's cleaning path or asking your robotic assistant to fetch something. It bridges the gap between technology and natural human interaction.

Steps
1. Pair robot to a voice assistant device.
2. Set up custom commands.
3. Regularly update and test voice modules.
4. Train voice recognition for accuracy.

Practical Challenges
Voice recognition might misinterpret commands. A command to clean the living room might have the robot vacuum go to the dining room, for example.

Tactics to Overcome
Ensure a quiet environment during initial voice training. Use distinct, clear commands. Regularly update software for enhanced recognition.

TIP 83: CRAFTED DRONE LANDING ZONES

Category
DIY Safety Enhancements

Brief
A custom landing pad ensures drones have a clear, debris-free spot, reducing wear and tear. In daily scenarios like beach outings or forest adventures, such pads prevent sand or dirt from affecting drone components. It's a proactive step to elongate drone life and ensure safer landings.

Steps
1. Choose a flat, wide material like cloth or rubber.
2. Mark with visible patterns.
3. Secure with weights or pegs during use.

Practical Challenges
Landing in uneven terrains might still pose challenges. In windy conditions, without proper securing, the landing pad could shift, causing misalignment.

Tactics to Overcome
Use contrasting colors for visibility. Regularly inspect and clean the pad. Always ensure it's well-secured before drone flights.

TIP 84: DISTINCTIVE DRONE ALERTS

Category
Sound Customization

Brief
Drones, when out of sight, can alert users through custom sounds, indicating low battery or loss of signal. It's crucial during mountain treks or beach filming when distractions abound. These distinct alerts can prevent potential drone losses or crashes.

Steps
1. Access drone sound settings.
2. Choose or upload distinct sounds.
3. Test alerts before actual flights.

Practical Challenges
Surrounding noises might overshadow these alerts. For instance, during a beach party, the drone's alert might go unnoticed amidst the music and chatter.

Tactics to Overcome
Opt for loud, sharp sounds. Regularly check drone volume settings. Combine sound alerts with visual (LED) alerts for redundancy.

TIP 85: DRONE SAFETY BOUNDARIES

Category
Geofencing

Brief
Setting up geofences ensures drones don't venture into restricted zones, be it near airports or private properties. It's a boon for daily drone users who might unintentionally breach airspace rules. It acts as an invisible safety net, ensuring drones operate within set confines, avoiding potential legal issues.

Steps
1. Access drone mapping software.
2. Mark safe operation zones.
3. Save and activate geofencing.

Practical Challenges
GPS inaccuracies might cause boundary overlaps. In real-life scenarios, a drone might stop operations a few meters before an actual boundary due to GPS drift.

Tactics to Overcome
Regularly update drone GPS modules. Cross-check geofence boundaries with local regulations and maps. Adjust boundaries considering a margin for GPS inaccuracies.

TIP 86: MODULAR ROBOT ENHANCEMENTS

Category
Hardware Customization

Brief
By adding modular components like additional arms, cameras, or tools, users can expand a robot's functionalities. For instance, a robotic pet can have added sensors for interaction, or a robotic helper might have a new tool attachment for gardening tasks. It provides flexibility and versatility to robot owners, adapting to changing needs.

Steps
1. Determine desired functionality.
2. Purchase or build the compatible module.
3. Attach and calibrate the new module to the robot.
4. Test its operations thoroughly.

Practical Challenges
Module incompatibility can arise, leading to malfunctions. For instance, an aftermarket camera might drain too much power from a robot designed for minimal energy use.

Tactics to Overcome
Only use manufacturer-approved modules or ensure compatibility specs match. Regularly monitor robot health and performance after adding new components.

TIP 87: DRONE LIGHT CUSTOMIZATIONS

Category
Aesthetic Enhancements

Brief
Adding custom LED lights or patterns to drones not only beautifies them but can be functional, aiding in night flights or visibility in foggy conditions. It's useful for users who often fly at dusk or dawn, ensuring their drone stands out against the backdrop and is easily traceable.

Steps
1. Decide the lighting pattern and placement.
2. Choose lightweight, energy-efficient LEDs.
3. Install them, ensuring no interference with drone functions.
4. Test fly in different lighting conditions.

Practical Challenges
Increased power consumption or added weight can affect flight times or stability. In real scenarios, a drone might have reduced flight duration due to heavy lighting modules.

Tactics to Overcome
Opt for lightweight and energy-efficient LEDs. Check drone's balance post-installation. Monitor battery usage during initial flights to gauge the impact.

CHAPTER 12 - TABLET AND IPAD ENHANCEMENTS

TIP 88: MULTI-PURPOSE STAND

Category
Hardware Creation

Brief
In today's multitasking environment, a stand that serves more than one purpose, like charging and holding your stylus, can be incredibly beneficial. This trick ensures tablets are always ready for use, enhancing productivity. This stand ensures that in daily tasks, be it meetings or personal browsing, your device stays accessible and charged.

Steps
1. Choose a sturdy material like wood.
2. Design spaces for charging and stylus holding.
3. Assemble and place in a convenient location.

Practical Challenges
A common challenge might be finding the right design that suits all devices and complements room aesthetics. A user might find it tough ensuring stability with larger tablets.

Tactics to Overcome
Opt for adjustable designs. If DIY, consider consulting basic carpentry guides to enhance stability and aesthetics. Periodically check for wear and tear.

TIP 89: ICON COHESION

Category
Software Personalization

Brief
For those who thrive in organized environments, having cohesive app icons can bring visual satisfaction and enhanced usability. Uniform icons mean less visual clutter, speeding up task initiation. Daily, as one opens their tablet, this clean layout can boost mood and task efficiency.

Steps
1. Choose or design a uniform icon theme.
2. Apply via personalization apps or tablet settings.
3. Rearrange icons for optimal usability.

Practical Challenges
A challenge is ensuring all app icons fit the chosen theme. Some apps might not allow changes, leading to occasional outliers.

Tactics to Overcome
Use third-party apps that allow for broader customization. Accept minor inconsistencies, focusing on the overall cohesive look.

TIP 90: PROTECTIVE UTILITY CASE

Category
Hardware Enhancement

Brief
A protective case that also has pockets or slots for cards, notes, or a stylus provides added functionality. It ensures safety while also making daily tasks more streamlined by keeping essentials close. During meetings or travel, having everything in one place can be incredibly time-saving.

Steps
1. Identify required utilities.
2. Purchase or design a case that fulfills these.
3. Regularly declutter and organize the utilities.

Practical Challenges
One might find it bulky with all utilities in. Overloading can also wear out the case faster.

Tactics to Overcome
Prioritize essentials, avoid overstuffing. Opt for cases made of durable materials and periodically inspect for signs of wear.

TIP 91: QUICK SWIPE GESTURES

Category
Software Enhancement

Brief
Time is of the essence. By customizing swipe gestures, one can launch apps or tasks quicker. This is beneficial when multitasking or when quick access is needed, like during presentations. It seamlessly integrates into daily use, elevating efficiency and responsiveness.

Steps
1. Access gesture settings on the tablet.
2. Customize each gesture with desired actions.
3. Practice for muscle memory.

Practical Challenges
The challenge lies in remembering each customized gesture. Accidental swipes can also initiate unintended tasks.

Tactics to Overcome
Start with a few key gestures. Over time, as muscle memory builds, expand the list. Use clear, distinguishable gestures.

TIP 92: ERGONOMIC STYLUS GRIP

Category
Hardware Creation

Brief
An ergonomic grip ensures prolonged stylus use without discomfort. It's particularly useful for artists or note-takers who use the tablet extensively. This trick can make daily work sessions more comfortable, preventing hand strains and enhancing work quality.

Steps
1. Measure stylus thickness.
2. Choose a comfortable, cushioned material.
3. Design and attach to the stylus.

Practical Challenges
Finding the perfect grip size can be tricky. Too thick might be as uncomfortable as too thin.

Tactics to Overcome
Start with adjustable grips, modify based on comfort. Periodically replace if wear is noticed.

TIP 93: SHORTCUT MASTERY

Category
Software Efficiency

Brief
Keyboards can be personalized with shortcuts for frequent phrases or tasks, saving time. Daily communications or repetitive tasks become swifter. For professionals or students, this can significantly speed up task completions.

Steps
1. Identify frequently used phrases or tasks.
2. Assign them to specific shortcuts.
3. Regularly use and review for efficiency.

Practical Challenges
Remembering all shortcuts can be daunting. Over-customization might lead to confusion.

Tactics to Overcome
Keep a handy list initially. Start with vital shortcuts, gradually increasing as you become comfortable.

TIP 94: SCREEN SPLIT MASTERY

Category
Software Productivity

Brief
Efficient multitasking requires rapid switching between apps. Using screen split effectively can make daily tasks, like comparing documents or watching a tutorial while taking notes, significantly smoother. This trick amplifies productivity and task management.

Steps
1. Open desired apps.
2. Activate screen split from settings or gesture.
3. Resize based on preference.

Practical Challenges
Some apps might not support split-screen. Managing screen real estate with multiple apps can be challenging.

Tactics to Overcome
Familiarize with apps supporting split view. Prioritize based on task importance and adjust screen ratios accordingly.

TIP 95: NOTIFICATION TUNES

Category
Software Personalization

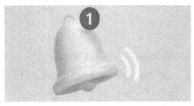

Brief
Tailored notification sounds for different apps or contacts can be both fun and functional. It aids in prioritizing attention without even looking at the screen. In daily scenarios, recognizing an important email or message sound can aid in timely responses.

Steps
1. Identify key apps or contacts.
2. Assign unique sounds from settings.
3. Regularly review and update.

Practical Challenges
Over-customizing can lead to confusion, forgetting which sound corresponds to which app.

Tactics to Overcome
Limit customization to primary apps or contacts. Keep a list or legend initially until familiar.

CHAPTER 13 - PERSONALIZING CAR TECH

TIP 96: INFOTAINMENT CUSTOMIZATION

Category
Car Infotainment

Brief
Modern cars come with sophisticated infotainment screens, but many use default backgrounds. Custom backgrounds not only add a personal touch but also make the interface more visually appealing. Especially during long rides, a personalized background can create a cozy atmosphere. In daily commutes, seeing a favorite photo or theme could even brighten up one's mood.

Steps
1. Choose a high-res image.
2. Save to USB drive.
3. Plug USB into car.
4. Access infotainment settings. 5. Choose option to change background. 6. Select image from USB.

Practical Challenges
Some cars might not support this feature or have limited file format support. Additionally, overly bright or flashy images might distract the driver. In the worst case, a wrong step could reset the entire infotainment system.

Tactics to Overcome
Ensure your car's model supports this feature. Always have a backup of your system. Choose subtle images that won't distract.

TIP 97: DIY AMBIENT CAR LIGHTS

Category
Car Lighting

 **Brief**
Ambient car lighting can give your vehicle a futuristic look, while also being functional during nighttime driving. It can enhance the mood, make controls more visible, and personalize the car environment. Whether it's serene blues or fiery reds, lighting can change the entire ambiance of the vehicle. Daily, during evening rides or long journeys, they can provide solace and even decrease driving fatigue.

Steps
1. Purchase LED strip lights.
2. Choose desired color scheme.
3. Install under dashboard and seats.
4. Connect to car battery or cigarette lighter. 5. Use remote or app to adjust colors.

Practical Challenges
There might be issues with wiring or connecting to the power source. The LED strips might not adhere well to some surfaces or may interfere with car functions. Continuous use might drain the car battery faster.

Tactics to Overcome
Opt for professional installation if unsure. Ensure lights don't interfere with driving. Periodically check battery health.

TIP 98: VOICE ROUTE COMMANDS

Category
Navigation

Brief
Modern cars have integrated voice command systems. Personalizing voice commands for frequent routes can save time and make daily commutes smoother. Instead of manually setting the destination daily, imagine saying, "Go to work," and your car sets the route instantly. This is invaluable for daily office commutes, dropping kids at school, or weekend getaways. It streamlines the driving experience, making navigation hassle-free.

Steps
1. Access car's navigation system.
2. Save frequent destinations.
3. Set personalized voice commands for each.
4. Test by giving the voice command.

Practical Challenges
Setting accurate voice commands can be tricky. Some systems may not recognize specific accents or pronunciations. Misunderstood commands might set wrong destinations.

Tactics to Overcome
Train the system with clear pronunciations. Use short, distinct phrases. Update the system regularly.

TIP 99: CUSTOM EQ FOR CAR AUDIO

Category
Sound Systems

Brief
Cars usually come with default equalizer (EQ) settings, which may not always provide the best sound for every genre of music. Custom EQ settings can greatly enhance audio quality based on individual preferences. Perfect for audiophiles or anyone wanting to get the best sound experience in their daily drives or road trips. It can turn mundane drives into immersive musical journeys.

Steps
1. Access car audio settings.
2. Navigate to EQ settings.
3. Adjust frequencies as per preference.
4. Save the custom setting. 5. Test with various songs.

Practical Challenges
Some users might find adjusting frequencies challenging. Default settings may sound distorted on some tracks. Over-amplification might damage the speakers.

Tactics to Overcome
Start with genre-specific presets. Gradually adjust frequencies. Avoid excessive bass or treble.

TIP 100: CUSTOM BOOT ANIMATIONS

Category
Car Display

Brief
A custom boot animation on your car's display adds a personal touch every time you start the vehicle. It's a daily reminder of your personal touch to the machine, creating a sense of ownership. For those who treat their car as more than just a transport medium, this makes every drive special.

Steps
1. Research if your car model supports custom animations.
2. Choose/create a suitable animation.
3. Save on a USB drive.
4. Upload via car's infotainment system.

Practical Challenges
Compatibility might be an issue. The wrong file format or size might lead to display errors. Animations might slow down the boot-up time.

Tactics to Overcome
Ensure the animation is optimized for your car. Keep a backup of the original. Regularly update the infotainment system.

TIP 101: INFOTAINMENT MAKEOVER

Category
Car Tech

Brief
Using unique infotainment backgrounds can give your car's dashboard a personalized look and make your driving experience more enjoyable. It's a simple tweak that can make a big difference. These backgrounds can mirror your mood, style, or even showcase a beloved family picture. Imagine starting your car and being greeted with your favorite vacation photo. This visual upgrade not only enhances aesthetic appeal but makes your car feel more "yours".

Steps
1. Save the desired image on a USB drive.
2. Insert the USB into the car's port.
3. Navigate to settings and select 'Change Infotainment Background'.
4. Choose the image from the USB.

Practical Challenges
Changing the infotainment background might void warranty or lead to issues with display readability during certain times of the day.

Tactics to Overcome
Make sure to check warranty conditions. Use high-contrast images that don't hinder display visibility.

TIP 102: DIY AMBIENT MOOD LIGHTING

Category
Car Tech

Brief
Adding DIY ambient lighting in your car can set the mood for your drives. Whether you want a calming blue for nighttime drives or a vibrant red for energetic morning commutes, ambient lighting can be both practical and aesthetic. It aids in visibility during night drives and adds a personal touch to your vehicle's interior.

Steps
1. Purchase LED strip lights.
2. Measure and cut the desired length.
3. Use the adhesive to place under dashboards, seats, or doors.
4. Connect to the car's electrical system.

Practical Challenges
Installing lights might be tricky for non-tech-savvy people. The adhesive could damage the car's original interior finish.

Tactics to Overcome
Opt for removable adhesives. Consult or hire a professional for electrical connections to avoid mishaps.

TIP 103: VOICE-ACTIVATED SHORTCUTS

Category
Car Tech

Brief
Instead of inputting frequent routes manually, set personal voice commands. It's not just about convenience, but safety as it reduces distraction. Imagine saying "Drive to work" and your navigation sets the course automatically. This feature is a boon, especially during busy mornings or when you're in unfamiliar territories.

Steps
1. Go to the car's voice command settings.
2. Select 'Add New Command'.
3. Input the destination and assign a custom phrase.

Practical Challenges
Different ambient noises might interfere with the system's ability to accurately catch commands.

Tactics to Overcome
Regularly update the system's software. Speak clearly and choose unique phrases that the system can easily recognize.

TIP 104: TAILORED AUDIO EXPERIENCE

Category
Car Tech

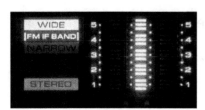

Brief
Tailoring your car's sound equalizer settings based on the music genre you prefer can significantly enhance audio quality. It can transform ordinary drives into immersive musical journeys. From boosting bass for electronic tracks to enhancing vocals for podcasts, tailored settings make a world of difference.

Steps
1. Go to audio settings.
2. Navigate to 'Equalizer'.
3. Adjust the bands according to preference.
4. Save the settings for future use.

Practical Challenges
Settings might revert post software updates or not save correctly at times.

Tactics to Overcome
Regularly backup settings. Avoid extreme tweaks which might distort sound or harm speakers.

CHAPTER 14 - UNIQUE MODS FOR SMART APPLIANCES

TIP 105: SMART OVEN COOKING DIARY

Category
Smart Ovens

Brief
Creating a personalized cooking routine using your smart oven can transform your culinary experience. By tailoring preset temperatures and cooking times for your favorite dishes, you save time and ensure consistent results. This trick is useful for families with fixed meal plans or individuals who love experimenting with recipes. Having a digital diary in your oven streamlines the cooking process, leading to enhanced time management and predictability in meal preps.

Steps
- List out favorite dishes.
- Set specific temperatures and cooking times.
- Label each entry appropriately.
- Test and adjust as needed.

Practical Challenges
Changing preferences or recipe alterations can lead to preset mismatches. An example is when you're trying a different pie recipe which requires a varied cooking time.

Tactics to Overcome
Periodically review and update presets. Experiment with a new dish multiple times before setting it in the oven's memory. Always have a backup manual timer to double-check.

TIP 106: LAUNDRY REMINDER SYSTEM

Category
Laundry Appliances

Brief
Sometimes we forget the laundry, leading to clothes that sit wet or become wrinkled. Tailored alerts can notify you precisely when a cycle ends, ensuring you always attend to your laundry promptly. This trick aids those with busy routines who often multitask. Prompt laundry management prevents clothes damage and saves time on ironing or redoing wash cycles.

Steps
- Set up laundry machine's smart app.
- Customize notification preferences.
- Sync with smartphones or smart home systems.

Practical Challenges
Tech glitches could cause missed alerts. For instance, Wi-Fi issues might prevent a notification from coming through.

Tactics to Overcome
Ensure a stable Wi-Fi connection. As a backup, set a standard timer or alarm on your phone coinciding with the average laundry cycle duration.

TIP 107: FRIDGE ART

Category
Smart Fridges

Brief
Turn your fridge into a piece of art! DIY decorative stickers not only enhance aesthetics but can also serve functional purposes like labeling sections. This tip is for those wanting to add a personal touch to their kitchen, making the fridge a centerpiece. This not only elevates the kitchen's look but can also serve as a conversation starter, contributing positively to home aesthetics.

Steps
- Measure fridge's surface area.
- Choose or design a sticker.
- Clean the surface.
- Carefully apply the sticker.

Practical Challenges
Stickers might leave residue, or design trends can change, leading to a mismatched kitchen aesthetic.

Tactics to Overcome
Opt for high-quality, easy-to-remove stickers. Regularly update or rotate designs to keep the fridge looking fresh and in sync with the rest of the kitchen.

TIP 108: VOICE BREW COMMAND

Category
Coffee Makers

Brief
Start your morning effortlessly with a custom voice recipe for your smart coffee maker. Tailor the strength, size, and type of your coffee. Ideal for those groggy mornings when manually operating appliances feels tedious. It ensures a consistent coffee taste every morning, uplifting your mood and kickstarting your day.

Steps
- Record the voice command.
- Set coffee preferences.
- Test the command.
- Adjust for precision.

Practical Challenges
Accidental activation or misinterpretation of voice commands could lead to unwanted brewing. Imagine mistakenly preparing a strong coffee late at night.

Tactics to Overcome
Regularly recalibrate voice recognition for accuracy. Set a time frame when voice activation is off to prevent accidental brewing.

TIP 109: ROBO-VAC SCHEDULER

Category
Robotic Vacuums

Brief
Program your robo-vac to clean at specific times, focusing on high-traffic areas during the week and a full house sweep on weekends.
Perfect for maintaining a consistently clean home without daily intervention. Scheduled cleaning prevents dirt buildup, providing a healthier living environment and a cleaner aesthetic appeal.

Steps
- Map out your home's layout on the robo-vac app.
- Set cleaning times.
- Designate specific areas for each schedule.

Practical Challenges
Furniture movement or new obstacles might confuse the robo-vac. For instance, a new rug might get caught in the vacuum during its cleaning cycle.

Tactics to Overcome
Do weekly checks to ensure the home layout in the app matches reality. Update the robot's map regularly and ensure the floor is free of small items that could become obstacles.

TIP 110: MAINTENANCE ALERTS

Category
All Smart Appliances

Brief
Regular maintenance ensures longevity. Personalized reminders can be set for filter changes, software updates, or general checks. Essential for those with multiple smart devices. Staying on top of maintenance prevents potential malfunctions, saving money and ensuring consistent performance.

Steps
- List all smart appliances.
- Research each device's maintenance needs.
- Set reminders accordingly.

Practical Challenges
Forgetting to act upon an alert might lead to long-term damage. An overlooked oven maintenance reminder could result in uneven cooking in the future.

Tactics to Overcome
Besides digital reminders, have a physical calendar or board in a frequently visited area like the kitchen. Mark important maintenance dates to ensure they're not overlooked.

TIP 111: MOOD REFLECTING MIRRORS

Category
Smart Mirrors

Brief
Smart mirrors can be tailored to project mood lighting based on time or user preference. Warm lighting during evenings or cool during mornings can simulate natural light patterns, benefiting mental well-being. This trick enhances daily routines, making mundane tasks like brushing teeth a more immersive experience.

Steps
- Set up the smart mirror's controls.
- Program desired lighting patterns.
- Adjust based on user feedback.

Practical Challenges
Relying solely on mood lighting might distort makeup application or shaving precision in the mornings.

Tactics to Overcome
Integrate a manual override switch for natural white light when precision tasks are being performed. Balance between mood enhancement and practicality.

TIP 112: DIY KITCHEN GADGET HOLDERS

Category
Smart Kitchen Gadgets

Brief
Craft personalized holders for your smart kitchen gadgets. Using materials like wood or recycled items adds a touch of creativity. Perfect for those who want a unique kitchen setup. Such accessories reduce countertop clutter, making the kitchen more functional and aesthetically pleasing.

Steps
- Identify gadgets needing holders.
- Measure dimensions.
- Design and craft the holders.

Practical Challenges
Incorrect measurements or material choices could lead to holders that don't fit or damage the gadgets. A wooden holder might retain moisture, affecting the gadget's functionality.

Tactics to Overcome
Ensure precise measurements. Opt for moisture-resistant materials. Place silicone or rubber pads at the base of holders for added protection.

CHAPTER 15 - SMARTWATCH AND FITNESS BAND OVERHAUL

TIP 113: DYNAMIC GOAL ADJUSTMENT

Category
Customized Activity Goals

Brief
Dynamic Goal Adjustment allows users to flexibly change activity goals based on personal needs and daily conditions. Why? Because not all days are the same. On some days, one might feel energetic and on others, one might need rest. By adjusting goals, users get a personalized approach to fitness. For instance, after a marathon, instead of the usual 10k steps, one can set a 5k step goal. This ensures continued motivation and avoids burnout.

Steps
1. Open smartwatch settings.
2. Navigate to activity goals.
3. Adjust using sliding bar.
4. Confirm and sync.

Practical Challenges
One major challenge is overestimating or underestimating one's capacity. For example, setting a goal too high can be demotivating. Conversely, a goal set too low can lead to underperformance.

Tactics to Overcome
Instead of manually adjusting daily, use historical data and mood trackers. This provides a balanced and data-driven goal that's both challenging and achievable.

TIP 114: WATCH FACE CRAFTING 101

Category
Unique Watch Face Design Creation

Brief
Custom watch faces not only offer a personal touch but also enhance accessibility and functionality. Need to frequently check a specific timezone? Or perhaps, you're a stock trader who needs constant updates? Creating a tailored watch face ensures your top priorities are always in sight. For everyday use, having weather, calendar events, and top contacts can streamline activities.

Steps
1. Access the watch face store or editor.
2. Choose from existing designs or start from scratch.
3. Add widgets of choice.
4. Adjust color and style. 5. Save and set as default.

Practical Challenges
The dilemma is overcluttering. With endless widgets, one can easily make the watch face too busy, defeating the purpose of quick glances.

Tactics to Overcome
Limit to 3-4 essential widgets. Use color coding and grouping to keep the design clean and functional. This way, you get quick access without the visual overload.

TIP 115: PERSONAL TRAINER ON THE WRIST

Category
Tailored Workout Routines

Brief
Smartwatches are like personal trainers. However, a one-size-fits-all approach doesn't work for fitness. By customizing workouts, users get routines that cater to specific needs, such as rehab exercises post-injury or prenatal workouts. It's essential for those who need a routine matching their daily energy and health levels. For instance, during flu season, a lighter routine can prevent overexertion.

Steps
1. Go to the workout app.
2. Choose "Create New Routine".
3. Add exercises based on preference.
4. Set duration and intensity. 5. Save and start anytime.

Practical Challenges
Creating a balanced routine is challenging. Over-focusing on one muscle group can lead to imbalances. Similarly, misjudging one's capacity can result in injuries.

Tactics to Overcome
Ensure routines are well-rounded. Rotate between strength, flexibility, and cardio. Seek guidance from fitness apps that offer balance and structure.

TIP 116: FUNCTION MEETS FASHION

Category
DIY Watch Bands with Added Functionality

Brief
Watch bands can be more than style statements. By integrating tools like mini compasses or adding pouches for keys, they can be functional aids, especially for runners or hikers. This brings convenience, such as having a mini-toolkit on the wrist or a slot for emergency cash.

Steps
1. Choose a durable watch band.
2. Decide on added elements like pouches, tools, etc.
3. Sew or attach securely.
4. Ensure comfort isn't compromised.

Practical Challenges
Balancing aesthetics with functionality is tricky. A heavily-loaded band might be useful but can become cumbersome or uncomfortable.

Tactics to Overcome
Prioritize based on frequency of use. Integrate elements that align with daily activities or specific adventures. Keep a balance to maintain comfort.

TIP 117: MUTED ALERTS SYSTEM

Category
Personalized Notification Filters

Brief
Constant notifications can be distracting. A tailored filter ensures only vital alerts come through during specific activities. It's indispensable when focusing on tasks, during meetings, or workouts. By filtering, one gets the peace of mind knowing they'll only be alerted for priority matters.

Steps
1. Access notification settings.
2. Prioritize apps or contacts.
3. Set "Do Not Disturb" schedules.
4. Sync and activate.

Practical Challenges
Over-filtering might lead to missing out on essential notifications. There's a risk of becoming too isolated or unresponsive.

Tactics to Overcome
Review and adjust filters weekly. Ensure a balance between staying focused and being accessible. Activate vibration alerts for semi-priorities.

TIP 118: OPTIMAL REST ANALYSIS

Category
Exclusive Sleep Tracking Settings

Brief
Sleep is vital. However, not all deep sleeps are restorative. By tweaking sleep settings, one can get insights into optimal rest periods, REM cycles, etc. This assists in identifying best bedtime hours and wake-up times. Perfect for those striving for peak productivity and mental clarity.

Steps
1. Navigate to sleep tracking settings.
2. Adjust tracking sensitivity if needed.
3. Set reminders for optimal bedtime.
4. Review data regularly.

Practical Challenges
Relying solely on trackers might lead to anxiety or over-analysis. One might get too focused on numbers rather than listening to their body.

Tactics to Overcome
While data is insightful, combine it with personal feelings upon waking. Ensure tracker settings match individual sleep patterns for accurate data.

TIP 119: HEALTH ALERT CUSTOMIZATION

Category
Tailored Health Monitoring Alerts

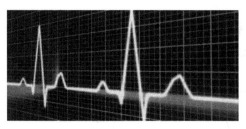

Brief
Health alerts, like abnormal heart rates or inactivity reminders, can be lifesavers. However, some generic thresholds might not apply to everyone. By customizing, one ensures alerts are in line with personal health profiles, avoiding unnecessary panics or overlooks.

Steps
1. Go to health monitoring settings.
2. Adjust alert thresholds.
3. Set reminders for medications or stretches if needed.
4. Sync and keep updated.

Practical Challenges
Generic settings might trigger false alarms or miss crucial signals. For instance, an athlete might have a resting heart rate lower than the average.

Tactics to Overcome
Regularly update profiles with recent health check-ups. Seek advice from healthcare professionals when setting thresholds. Ensure it reflects individual health metrics.

TIP 120: VOICE-POWERED EFFICIENCY

Category
Personal Voice Commands for Quick Actions

Brief
Voice commands provide swift access to features without scrolling. By customizing, one can set unique phrases for frequent actions. Perfect for on-the-go situations, like starting a workout or setting a reminder without stopping. It's hands-free efficiency at its best.

Steps
1. Navigate to voice command settings.
2. Record or set desired phrases.
3. Map each phrase to an action.
4. Test for accuracy and adjust as needed.

Practical Challenges
Misinterpretation of commands can lead to errors. Background noise might interfere, leading to inaccurate actions.

Tactics to Overcome

Ensure phrases are clear and distinct. Test in various environments to ensure robustness. Regularly update for accuracy and efficiency.

ABOUT THE AUTHOR

Step into the world of Anand, and you're in for a journey beyond just tech and algorithms. While his accolades in the tech realm are numerous, including penning various tech-centric and personal improvement ebooks, there's so much more to this multi-faceted author.

At the heart of Anand lies an AI enthusiast and investor, always on the hunt for the next big thing in artificial intelligence. But turn the page, and you might find him engrossed in a gripping cricket match or passionately cheering for his favorite football team. His weekends? They might be spent experimenting with a new recipe in the kitchen, penning down his latest musings, or crafting a unique design that blends creativity with functionality.

While his professional journey as a Solution Architect and AI Consultant, boasting over a decade of AI/ML expertise, is impressive, it's the fusion of this expertise with his diverse hobbies that makes Anand's writings truly distinctive.

So, as you navigate through his works, expect more than just information. Prepare for stories interwoven with passion, experiences peppered with life's many spices, and wisdom that transcends beyond the tech realm. Dive in and discover Anand, the author, the enthusiast, the chef, the sports lover, and above all, the storyteller.